Crafts

Betsey Chessen
Pamela Chanko

Scholastic Inc.
New York • Toronto • London • Auckland • Sydney

Acknowledgments

Literacy Specialist: Linda Cornwell

Social Studies Consultant: Barbara Schubert, Ph.D.

Design: Silver Editions

Photo Research: Silver Editions

Endnotes: Jacqueline Smith

Endnote Illustrations: Anthony Carnabucia

———————————————————

Photographs: Cover: David Sutherland/Tony Stone Images; p. 1: (tl) Glen Allison/Tony Stone Images; (tr) Bushnell/Soifer/Tony Stone Images; (bl) Jeff Greenberg/Photo Edit; (br) Martha Cooper/The Viesti Collection; p. 2: David Sutherland/Tony Stone Images; p. 3: James Strachan/Tony Stone Images; p. 4: Fujifotos/The Image Works; pp. 5, 6: Michael Newman/Photo Edit; p. 7: Joe Viesti/The Viesti Collection; p. 8: M. B. Duda/Photo Researchers, Inc.; p. 9: Renee Lynn/Photo Researchers, Inc.; p. 10: John Eastcott/The Image Works; p. 11: M. Douglas/The Image Works; p. 12: (tl) John Beatty/Tony Stone Images; (tr) Lory Karol/Gamma Liaison; (bl) Tony Freeman/Photo Edit; (br) Anna E. Zuckerman/Photo Edit

Library of Congress Cataloging-in-Publication Data
Chessen, Betsey, 1970-
Crafts/Betsey Chessen, Pamela Chanko.
p.cm. -- (Social studies emergent readers)
Summary: Simple text and photographs explore how artists around the world make their crafts, including weaving, calligraphy, and papier-mâché.
ISBN 0-439-04568-1 (pbk.: alk. paper)
1. Handicraft--Juvenile literature. [1. Handicraft.]
I. Chanko, Pamela, 1968-. II. Title. III. Series.
TT160.C523 1999

745.5--dc21

98-53337
CIP AC

7   8   9   10   08   08   07   06   05

These are crafts from around the world.

How were these rugs made?

By weaving.

How were these signs made?

By writing calligraphy.

How were these piñatas made?

By papier-mâché.

How was this pottery made?

By shaping clay.

How were these eggs made?

By painting.

People make crafts around the world.

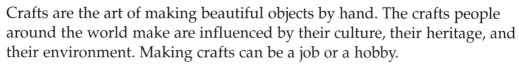

Crafts

Crafts are the art of making beautiful objects by hand. The crafts people around the world make are influenced by their culture, their heritage, and their environment. Making crafts can be a job or a hobby.

Indonesia's famous batik is made by drawing patterns on cloth with wax. The cloth is dipped in dye, and the wax is then scraped off. The process is repeated with other colors to make a richly patterned cloth. Japanese kites are admired for their interesting designs and shapes, their huge size, and their ability to fly very high. Kites in Japan have different meanings; for example, a dragon kite brings good luck. Stained glass is often found in church windows. It takes a lot of skill and time to create the design, make the colored glass, cut it into the shapes needed for the design, and then join the pieces with strips of lead. Handwoven rugs from Iran are world famous for their high quality and artistry. Iranians have developed this art for 2,500 years: They were some of the first rug weavers in the world.

Weaving Weaving is a very old craft. Nowadays it is done mostly on mechanical looms, but this Guatemalan woman is making a rug using the same techniques her ancestors did 2,000 years ago. She straps the loom around her waist with a belt and ties the other end onto a tree. She passes a shuttle, a piece of wood with thread attached, from one side of the loom to the other. Guatemalan weavers use brightly colored wool and ancient designs based on animals, plants, or the stars.

Calligraphy This word means "beautiful writing," but in Japan calligraphy is more like painting. The calligrapher uses a brush to "write" on paper or silk scrolls. The calligrapher finishes in seconds, but it is not as easy as it looks. He can write it only once—no corrections or additions—and he must get the thickness of the brushstrokes and the space between the words exactly right. It takes years of practice to do it well.

Papier-mâché In Mexico papier-mâché is used to make piñatas. The piñata maker mixes a paste of flour and water. He then tears newspapers into strips and dips them into the paste. He takes the soggy strips and pastes them onto a clay pot. When all the parts are dry, he decorates the piñata with tissue paper. Then he fills it with candies and little toys. Piñatas are hung on a rope for parties. Children are blindfolded and take turns whacking at the piñata with a long stick, trying to break it so that all the goodies fall out!

Pottery Potters were probably some of the earliest craftspeople: Archaeologists have found clay pots from 9,000 years ago! The Pueblo Indians have been using the same technique to make clay pots for 2,000 years. The potter takes clay and cleans it, grinds it, soaks it, and then rolls it into a rope. She coils the rope around on itself like a snake. She presses down on the coils, and when the pot is dry, she scrapes it, sands it, and then polishes it with a stone until it is smooth and shiny. She carves in a design or paints the clay with dyes. Finally she fires the pot in a homemade kiln—a very hot oven—to make it strong.

Ukrainian eggs The Ukrainians make decorated eggs a few weeks before the Christian holiday of Easter. Children use a special tool that they heat over a candle and then dip in beeswax. They draw fine lines of beeswax on the egg to make pictures. They then dip the egg in a light-color dye; the part under the wax does not absorb the color. They continue to draw on the egg and dip it into different colors, and finally they dip it in a dark color, like red or black. Next, the children warm the egg to melt the wax, which they then wipe off, and lacquer the multicolored egg to make it strong. Ukrainian eggs are "message eggs"—the pictures and colors all have special meanings. For instance, you might give an egg with wheat on it to a farmer to wish him a good harvest or one with a flower on it to someone you love.

Social Studies

EMERGENT READERS

Discover how artists make their crafts—from
weaving rugs to painting eggs.

ISBN 0-439-04568-1

9 780439 045681

90000

B